Self-Care for Ladies

The 7 Pillars of Self-Care and 100+ Wellness Activities for a Busy Professional Woman While She Cares for Her Family and Work

Marisa Strive

© Copyright 2022 - All rights reserved.

The content contained within this book may not be reproduced, duplicated or transmitted without direct written permission from the author or the publisher.

Under no circumstances will any blame or legal responsibility be held against the publisher, or author, for any damages, reparation, or monetary loss due to the information contained within this book, either directly or indirectly.

Legal Notice:

This book is copyright protected. It is only for personal use. You cannot amend, distribute, sell, use, quote or paraphrase any part, or the content within this book, without the consent of the author or publisher.

Disclaimer Notice:

Please note the information contained within this document is for educational and entertainment purposes only. All effort has been executed to present accurate, up to date, reliable, complete information. No warranties of any kind are declared or implied. Readers acknowledge that the author is not engaged in the rendering of legal, financial, medical or professional advice. The content within this book has been derived from various sources. Please consult a licensed professional before attempting any techniques outlined in this book.

By reading this document, the reader agrees that under no circumstances is the author responsible for any losses, direct or indirect, that are incurred as a result of the use of the information contained within this document, including, but not limited to, errors, omissions, or inaccuracies.

Table of Contents

INTRODUCTION 1

CHAPTER 1: WHY SELF-CARE IS IMPORTANT 7
    CHAPTER ACTIVITY: 14

CHAPTER 2: PHYSICAL SELF-CARE 17
    CHAPTER ACTIVITY: 33

CHAPTER 3: MENTAL SELF-CARE 35
    CHAPTER ACTIVITY: 44

CHAPTER 4: SENSORY SELF-CARE 45
    EYES 45
    NOSE 47
    EARS 49
    TONGUE 50
    SKIN 53
    CHAPTER ACTIVITY: 55

CHAPTER 5: CREATIVE SELF-CARE 57
    CHAPTER ACTIVITY: 62

CHAPTER 6: EMOTIONAL SELF-CARE 65
    CHAPTER ACTIVITY: 73

CHAPTER 7: SOCIAL SELF-CARE 75
    CHAPTER ACTIVITY: 81

CHAPTER 8: SPIRITUAL SELF-CARE 83
    MEDITATION 86
    YOGA 90

| Tai Chi | 92 |
| Chapter Activity: | 100 |

CONCLUSION **101**

REFERENCES **105**

Introduction

As you grow older, you will discover that you have two hands, one for helping yourself, the other for helping others. –Maya Angelou

Self-care is one of the most important yet most neglected habits. Self-care essentially means looking after one's physical, emotional, and mental health. It means to take actions which promote one's well-being and make one feel relaxed and happy. This habit benefit directly to the person practicing it and despite this, you will find most people neglect self-care and eventually it becomes an unhealthy routine. It is said that the best relationships are those in which both individuals are happy and secure in their own space. Only in this way can they participate in each other's happiness. Similarly, when we do not care for ourselves then we will never be able to rightly care for someone else. Unfortunately, even in today's day and age women are the main caregivers in a family, i.e, it is the women in a family who take care of everyone's needs. The women work and care for their kids, husband, and other family members; and because of so much burden most of the time, the women neglect themselves which only adds to the stress. This book aims to be a guide for all women who feel overwhelmed and are not able to give themselves the time and energy that is necessary for every human being.

My name is Marisa Strive and I am originally from Vietnam. I moved to Australia when I was a teenager and have been living there since. I am now in my thirties, married, and working as a full-time research scientist in the biotech industry. I am from a collective culture which means that from a very young age, I was taught to be responsible for my family. The happiness of my parents, grandparents, uncles, aunts, cousins, and even friends and teachers mattered more than my own. I always put others before myself and this habit became so ingrained in me that I felt that only putting others' needs above mine would mean that I mattered in people's lives. Eventually, I even started to do this in my relationships and my workplace. I started to give way more than I was receiving and subconsciously this started adding to my stress. A perfect society would be one where everyone lives with a mentality to give more than they receive and this leads to everyone being happy however, that is not the case in our world. Giving has always been an act of kindness but too much of anything can be toxic i.e if only one person is giving and never receiving back then it can be draining for that individual. I am a busy professional, I work with a team of scientists and my work includes managing multiple projects, writing technical reports, and performing analysis of blood for clinical trials amongst many other responsibilities. Before the COVID-19 pandemic hit us I was finishing my Ph.D. and I used to travel to Europe and America for scientific conferences and workshops where I met like-minded individuals working in the pharmaceutical sector. I have been a busy professional for most of my life and in all that I ignored myself and my needs. I feel that work should only be a chapter of a person's life and not their entire life. Like all of us, I feel responsible for my family and want to give them equal importance. I want to be a good daughter for my aging parents in Vietnam, a caring wife to my husband, a good friend, and a helpful colleague and in the future be a caring mother when I have children. However, for me to be able to do so I have to include myself in the list as well.

I received multiple scholarships throughout my educational journey in Australia and also got many opportunities to travel the world with supportive friends. I aim to be a responsible global citizen and a decent human being as well and give back as I feel a debt of gratitude. I try to do this by maintaining excellent work ethics, tutoring disadvantaged indigenous students over weekends, and also trying to gain new skills such as taking coding classes and an online business class. Due to the many commitments, I found myself sucked into filling the many responsibilities and somewhere forgetting myself. I used to take no breaks during work hours and used to even forget to eat or drink water the whole day. Then suddenly in March 2017, I had an episode of autoimmunity i.e my antibodies attacked my kidneys and started leaking proteins into urine and my entire body was swollen. I had to be admitted to the hospital immediately and that night even though I was sick lying in the hospital bed I realized that it was the calmest and most relaxed I had felt in a long time. And that was when I realized that I had pushed myself too hard all these years. I started to feel guilty because I had to cancel all my tutoring sessions with my students and even started feeling like a burden to the Australian healthcare system. I had become an extreme case of self-neglect but in retrospect, that night was like a blessing in disguise. I realized the importance of self-care and started practicing it diligently. I am now a more energetic, healthy, and happy individual, and feel that I can contribute more to society. My story goes to prove my earlier point that if we do not care for ourselves then we will never be able to rightly care for others.

It is a beautiful feeling to be able to care for others and many cultures teach us to always give more than we receive. While this is true and noble one must never neglect themselves in the process. I understand how overwhelming it can sometimes feel to have so many responsibilities. Sometimes, not being able to fulfill these responsibilities makes one feel guilty and helpless. However, I want anyone who feels this way to understand that you are only human in the end and we all deserve breaks and do not have to ever feel less of ourselves because we are unable to do something for someone.

Self-care differs for each individual, it should be a relaxing activity that one must enjoy and feel rejuvenated after. Self-care must not be another activity to tick under your to-do list but an activity that you love to do. Self-care can have different meanings for different women. For some, it might be a day's trek to the mountains and for others, it can be a regular pampering session at the salon. This book will be about the various forms of self-care and easy ways to practice them. Yes, self-care also has many forms, there is physical self-care, mental self-care, and even spiritual and creative self-care among others. I aim to give multiple options of self-care in this book so that each woman reading this book can choose the form of self-care that they most resonate with and start practicing them.

Through this book I want women to become the best version of themselves. I want that through my own experiences I can empower women to make themselves a priority. My own experience made me realize that there are numerous women out there who are going through a similar experience but have no one to guide them and I would like to be that guiding light for them. In this book, I have covered more than 100 self-care activities for women and they are divided into the many forms that I mentioned above. So leave all your worries behind and let's begin this beautiful journey together.

Chapter 1:

Why Self-Care Is Important

Women need solitude in order to find again the true essence of themselves. –Anne Morrow Lindbergh

I would like to begin this chapter with a very important word "Burnout." What is burnout? The dictionary definition of burnout is "Exhaustion of physical or emotional strength or motivation usually as a result of prolonged stress or frustration" (Merriam-Webster, 2019).

Burnout usually happens when a person has overworked, overburdened, and overloaded with various responsibilities without any break. In the corporate world, the best leaders are those who delegate tasks instead of burdening themselves with entire responsibilities. Similarly, in an ideal household situation, it should not just be only the woman who is burdened with the household responsibilities. A working woman must take the reins of her life and divide her household responsibilities equally. Just one person cannot be working, cooking, cleaning, and taking care of the family. While I will be sharing self-care tips I think it is very important to first establish the reasons why self-care is becoming necessary. If any person is burdened with many responsibilities then they most definitely would not be able to take time out for themselves which would ultimately lead to burnout.

In many cultures, women are conditioned to believe that it is their life goal to care for and raise a family. Many women feel like failures if they are unable to perform all the above duties and society increases these feelings within them. If a woman lives with her in-laws or other family members then they too can step in and give her a hand in the household chores. My own past tendency was to put everything else above myself be it my work or personal commitments and I learned only the hard way when all of this affected my physical health. To break these societal expectations and shackles women have to rise above and break these binding patterns that have been prevalent for generations. Traditionally women have been more nurturing but somewhere many of them became self-deprecating and started suffering from imposter syndrome. Imposter syndrome is when an individual doubts their skills and talents and feels like a fraud if they accomplish something. Self-care methods are like a cherry on the top of the cake but the main thing that women have to change first is their mindset and stop blaming themselves if they are unable to care for everyone. When we start to put ourselves on the top of our own list then everything else in our life will naturally fall into place.

The first safety instruction in an airplane is to wear one's own oxygen mask before trying and helping someone else put theirs on. Similarly, in life also, if we wish to care for our families and do well in our workplace the first step to doing that is to be the best version of ourselves and to care for ourselves first. Self-care does not have to be another to-do activity on your list, rather it should be an activity that you love to do and where time flows by while you are doing it. Another important step toward self-care is self-awareness. Self-awareness is when an individual introspects and becomes aware of their strengths, weakness, abilities, mistakes, and potential. Any self-aware person is already on a path to self-healing because they are aware of their flaws and can work to improve upon them. A self-aware person knows exactly where they need improvement and the path to self-care becomes much easier for them.

However, if you feel that you need help in determining your strengths and weaknesses then the first step for you to do is to introspect. Take a diary and write down your hobbies and passions, these are things you enjoy doing. Now think about where you can improve, we all have areas where we can improve and we just have to recognize them. Maybe you're someone who is an irritable driver or maybe you are always taking out flaws in everything, think of incidents where you regret your actions or words and now think of why you may have done them. For instance, taking the above example, if you are someone who is always criticizing and taking out flaws in other people then maybe you are the one who is not happy with where you are in life. Maybe it is your lack of effort that is coming out as irritation to other people. Once you recognize this you can now start to work on improving it. You only have to do this activity once and you will become very self-aware. Another thing that you can think about is triggers. What situations do you think trigger you and bring out a version of you that you are happy with? Think about this and if it is a particular individual let's say a friend, colleague, or family member then think why and what it is that they are doing that is triggering you. There are many benefits to being self-aware:

- Self-Confidence: A self-aware person recognizes their flaws and also their strengths. With self-awareness, a person becomes more aware of their emotions and they can then regulate them to see personal growth. A self-aware person works on their strengths and can even use them to choose a career that is right for them. Self-confidence does not only help in one's career but also in relationships.

- Growth: A self-aware person will focus on overcoming their weaknesses and will work on their strengths which will ultimately lead to the person's personal growth.

- Optimism: With self-awareness, a person gains clarity over their positive and negative thoughts. One can then work on turning the negative ones into positive ones which will lead a person to become more self-assured. This is because when a person gets the assurance that they are in control of their own emotions and thoughts then the person becomes unstoppable and gains confidence and clarity.

The diary activity mentioned above is a must for all those who wish to gain further clarity. However, there are a few more permanent solutions that will help a person become more self-aware:

- Yoga and Meditation: The core of yoga and meditation is to connect with oneself. There are various kinds of yoga and meditation techniques and now they can be easily found with just a touch on your smartphone. I would suggest guided meditation for beginners. Yoga and Meditation help in enhancing focus, reducing anxiety and depression symptoms, boost confidence, empathy, and happiness. We will delve deeper into this topic in further chapters as well.

- Another method is also regular journaling as it helps give clarity to thoughts and makes a person better aware of their strengths and weaknesses.

- Acknowledging one's feelings and triggers is one other important step to becoming more self-aware. When you self-reflect, remember to always be honest with yourself about your emotions, thoughts, and feelings.

A person can do as many self-care activities as they like but until the person does not conquer their own mind, they would never truly heal. Self-awareness is the key to happiness and we women must work to develop it.

In further chapters, we will be delving deeper into the seven types of self-care activity types but I would like to give you a brief introduction to them below:

- Physical Self-Care: The human body is like a temple and we must respect and care for it. Physical fitness does not only make your body healthy but it also keeps your mental health in check. Physical self-care involves regular exercising, eating healthy, drinking plenty of water, regularly taking a shower, soaking in sunlight, etc.

- Mental Self-Care: The mind's health is equally if not more important than physical health. It includes pursuing your hobbies/ passions, listening to music and podcasts, spending time with family and friends, watching movies, reading a book, journaling, practicing mindfulness and reflection.

- Sensory Self-Care: Sensory self-care takes into account all the senses which are smell, touch, vision, and sound. Self-care activities that include sensory self-care are aromatherapy, having a hot shower, taking a walk in nature, watching the sunrise and sunset, meditation, etc.

- Creative Self-Care: All human beings are creative. Some just need to be awakened. There are several activities in this particular self-care activity and a few of them include visualization, manifestation, cooking, singing/dancing in the shower, gardening, dancing, arts and crafts, and many more. Each person will be attracted to a different creative art and you just need to find one that speaks to you.

- Emotional Self-Care: Emotional health is also one of the most important and unfortunately most underrated self-care methods. A few of the methods include talking about your thoughts and feelings with a supportive friend, journaling, practicing gratitude, going for a relaxing hobby such as bird watching, photography, etc.

- Social Self-Care: We are social animals and we do need people to survive. Social self-care is all about catching up with your friends and spending time with them, chilling with your pet, going on a date, keeping in touch with your parents, etc.

- Spiritual Self-Care: Spiritual self-care includes meditation, prayer, yoga, reading a motivational book or listening to a motivational podcast.

There are numerous ways to practice each of the above self-care methods and I will be listing them down in further chapters as we explore each of them in detail. We do not realize it but our energy is dispersed throughout the day. Be it when you're answering your kids' questions, performing a duty in your job, socializing with your professional colleagues/clients, spending time with your spouses, or going out with your friends and family. We are constantly surrounded by other people's energies and it becomes almost a necessity to then give ourselves time. Self-care is often seen as a stigma or a selfish thing, however, it is far from it. When we put our needs before others we are indirectly helping other people by becoming the best versions of ourselves and this is what this book is about. I would now like to go into the different types of self-care and the ways we can practice them.

I will be giving an activity at the end of every chapter and hopefully, these can help you take the first steps in your self-care journey.

Chapter Activity:

The activity for this chapter is jotting down your wishes, your goals, your priorities, and details about your current life in a diary. Take out 15-20 minutes and think about each of these points. This will help you get clarity on the kind of life you wish to live in comparison with how you are currently living.

Read the paragraph below after completing the activity above:

You will notice that your priorities are everything from your children, partner, families, work, etc. and most of you will not even mention yourself. Well, by the end of this book, I will ensure this changes and will make sure that you naturally write self-care and self-love as the main priorities in your life.

Chapter 2:

Physical Self-Care

To love oneself is the beginning of a lifelong romance. –Oscar Wilde

Our bodies are the only faithful vehicle that enables you to go about doing your daily activities and chase your dreams, and stick with you through thick and thin and so it is quite important to feel fabulous in our bodies to enjoy the ride of life. The world will throw worries and tragedies at us but if we are comfortable and confident in our skin then nothing will stop us. Physical self-care is the most important habit that each person in this world should have. Being a physically fit person means that you have a healthy body, a healthy mind, and even healthy emotional health. I also want to reiterate that a physically fit person will be able to take better care of others and be a more valuable addition to society. Your physical self-care can take you to great heights in your career and the dedication and focus that physical fitness gives also has effects on one's relationships. It is very important for women to be fit as well because neglecting their physical health can make them more prone to physical illnesses such as PCOS, diabetes, heart problems, pregnancy problems, postmenopausal breast cancer, endometrial cancer, breathing problems, etc. which can lead to sleep apnea, high blood pressure, high cholesterol, anxiety, depression, hypertension and many more. It is seen very often that women will put their families i.e children and husband's health before their own and even if they feel exhausted they will keep going because they feel they will be failures if they do not. I would like to reiterate that this mentality needs to change and women need to understand that they are human too.

I would like to share below some of the best ways for you to get started on your physical self-care journey.

The first thing you should do after waking up is to drink water. You do not want to start your day dehydrated. It is recommended that adult women must consume at least 2.7 liters of water. Having an adequate amount of water daily results in:

- Increase in physical energy and performance.
- Can improve brain function which leads to better performance of daily tasks.
- Can help treat headaches.
- Prevent constipation.
- Helps in better functioning of the urinary system which prevents problems like kidney stones.
- Help in weight loss.
- Keeps the joints lubricated which helps prevent joint pains.

- Helps supply oxygen throughout the body through the blood which is 90% water.

- Dehydration can lead to skin problems and even early aging.

- Helps regulate body temperature.

- Aids in better functioning of the digestive system.

- Keeps blood pressure in check.

As you can see, this one small change in your lifestyle can improve the entire functioning of your body which can lead to amazing results.

My second point for you is to start planning your meals for the week in advance. Only use fresh produce and try and make every meal a rainbow meal i.e on the plate there should be leafy vegetables, grains, pulses, fruits, proteins, adequate carbohydrates, etc. it can differ for every person and all of the above do not necessarily have to be on every plate however, the motive is to put a little extra effort into your meals so that your plate looks colorful. For example, if you are having an omelet for breakfast then you can combine it with bell peppers, spinach, mushrooms, onions, etc. Or you can have a smoothie bowl with mangoes, raspberries, strawberries, blueberries, kiwis, or any fruit that you readily have available.

Every natural fruit and vegetable has vitamins and minerals required for the healthy functioning of the human body, so don't overthink and include whatever you have available in your meals. Some of the best vegetables with lots of nutrients include Spinach, carrots, garlic, broccoli, kale, Brussels sprouts, green peas, swiss chards, beetroot, asparagus, sweet potato, cauliflower, red peppers, tomatoes, onions, etc. Some of the best nutrient-filled fruits include Apples, bananas, blueberries, oranges, mangoes, avocado, dragon fruit, lychees, strawberries, pineapples, olives, durian, cherries, kiwis, watermelon, peaches, guava, grapes, pomegranates, grapefruits, etc. If there are other readily available fruits and vegetables in your region then please feel free to include them in your diet. Another tip I would like to share with you all is to eat as many raw fruits and vegetables as you can as cooking them does take out some of the nutrients.

Following the above tips and eating healthy meals leads to amazing benefits for your body such as:

- Helps boost immunity.
- Increases longevity.
- Keeps the skin glowing and healthy.
- Keeps the eyes, teeth, and other organs healthy and well functioning.
- Helps strengthen bones.
- Lowers risk of cancers and heart diseases.
- Aids in healthy pregnancies and breastfeeding.

- Maintains a healthy weight.

- Helps a person's digestive system.

- Keeps diabetes in control and can even prevent diabetes.

- Helps boost brain health.

- Can help improve mental health which leads to a reduction in stress levels as well.

- Helps in energy levels which leads to better performance at work.

- Also helps the environment as less processed foods such as fresh fruits and vegetables lead to sustainability.

Healthy eating doesn't necessarily mean boring eating. There are numerous ways to make your meals tasty and healthy. For example, you can avoid market-bought dressings for your salads and instead make them at your home sugar and fat-free but with the same fun taste. While you're on this, remember to also take breaks from healthy eating and binge on some cake, pizzas, or any other junk food as that is also self-care but remember to never go extreme.

The third and most important point is to make exercising a daily habit. Our body requires movement and taking out time for a daily exercise routine can do amazing benefits to the human body and it is the ultimate form of self-care. Exercising doesn't necessarily mean going to the gym and lifting heavy weights, it can be a walk/jog in the park, swimming, cycling, yoga, dance, home workouts, sports, Zumba, etc. The only way you can convince yourself to exercise daily is if you find out which exercise works best for you and is also something that you enjoy. Start with 15 minutes and then slowly increase to 30 minutes and 1 hour. You can even distribute 30 minutes to different types of exercises. For instance, maybe you like to play a particular sport so you can do that and then later practice yoga. Most of our work includes long sitting hours which leads to a sedentary lifestyle, something that is very harmful to the body. Did you know? In Australia, there is a culture of many working individuals exercising during their lunch breaks. As for the benefits of physical exercise? There are endless and include:

- It is the ultimate weapon for weight loss and weight management.

- It improves mood and hence, can lead to happiness.

- It increases energy levels which helps in one's job as well.

- Very good for the smooth functioning of one's muscles and bones.

- Reduce risks of having cholesterol, diabetes, heart attacks, etc.

- Aids in skin health.

- Excellent for mental health and brain functioning.

- Makes one more focused and determined.

- Improves sleep.

- Can lead to a healthy sex life.

- Great for one's self-esteem and confidence.

- Increases longevity.

Your exercise time can also become your me time where you listen to your favorite music, think about your day, and plan ahead. Do pick an exercise today and take the first step to a healthy body. You can start by joining a class or simply trying out a home workout video from YouTube.

The fourth point is to get an adequate amount of sleep. For an adult woman, 7 hours of everyday sleep is a must for a healthy functioning body and mind. Try and follow nature's routine of waking up and sleeping. Nowadays with the internet, people spend hours scrolling on their phones or watching Netflix and sleep very late at night. This does nothing but kill your dopamine levels. Instead, use this time to sleep properly and then follow your self-care routine. There are numerous benefits of an adequate amount of sleep:

- Helps maintain and lose weight.

- Improves productivity, energy levels, and concentration.
- Helps in the healthy functioning of the heart.
- Prevents diseases like diabetes and heart problems.
- Helps prevent depression.
- Keeps inflammation and the immune system healthy.
- Promotes wellness and leads to better results in school/college/workplace.

This particular self-care routine is doable and to promote this you can take a warm water bath before bedtime, read a nice book, have green tea, use essential oils/aroma candles, etc. all of these aid in relaxation which then leads to better sleep.

Some other activities for physical self-care include:

- Start practicing gratitude. Before going to bed right down five things that went well in the day.
- Go for pampering sessions at the salon or go for massages.
- Go out for a shopping day alone or with your friends.

- Plan evening parties such as game nights etc. with your friends and family.

- Go to the movies.

- Go on dates with your significant other.

- Spend quality time with the children or your pets.

- Take a five-minute break each day and sit with your thoughts. It's important to give yourself some me-time.

- Start meditation as it helps reduce anxiety, and depression and puts one in a great mood. You can start by chanting "om" or go for a meditation class. There are various kinds of meditations which we will be covering in the next few chapters.

- Write down any negative thoughts on paper and then beside them right down your reality.

- Start gardening or buy a new plant.

- Once a month go volunteering. It can be about any cause that you are passionate about. Be it helping the needy, animals, the environment, etc.

- Do not do anything you don't like i.e if you don't like to eat broccoli then don't. There are many other substitutes. Your life should be easy.

- Take a break from your job and technology. Go out into nature with your family.

- If you like to watch TV then do another activity with it, for example, lift weights or paint.

- Buy some amazing skin products such as a body lotion in your favorite scent, perfumes, etc. these all help a person feel better about themselves.

- Go on a vacation.

Physical self-care is vital and the above are fun things that you can easily take out time to do. I believe prevention is better than cure, and if prevention is so easy then why worry or stress? Start today and be happy.

While an overworking lifestyle can lead to a lack of self-care, I feel it is also very important to discuss the ill effects of a sedentary lifestyle. Oftentimes an individual can be so exhausted with work that they just want to come home and spend time in their beds. Most of our work is now on our computers and we end up sitting at our desks for more than eight to nine hours every day. We all must have heard of how important it is for one to exercise daily and especially nowadays. We have all unconsciously adopted a sedentary lifestyle which means sitting in one place for long periods. An average office-going person wakes up in the morning, goes to an office where they sit for an average of eight hours, and then comes back home to do little work and again sits on their bed and watches Netflix. The internet is addictive and most people now want to just sit at home and scroll on their phones or televisions instead of going out and meeting people. A sedentary lifestyle is one of the most toxic things that we can do for our bodies and minds.

There are numerous health risks involved in following this lifestyle and a few of them include

1. Makes one easily gain weight as one is burning next to zero calories. This also puts one at risk for obesity.

2. It can weaken your muscle strength as they are hardly being used. Similarly, one's bones can also get weaker due to a lack of mineral content.

3. One's metabolism can go down which will lead to the body facing difficulties in breaking down sugar and fats.

4. It can lead to a weaker immune system, disrupt healthy blood circulation, cause inflammation in the body, and ultimately even create a hormonal imbalance.

5. All of the above puts one at risk for diseases such as obesity, high blood pressure, high cholesterol, heart diseases such as heart attacks

and coronary artery diseases, diabetes, and cancers such as breast cancer, colon cancer, and uterine cancer. It can even cause and increase anxiety and depression in people.

The above are just some of the many diseases that can form because of a sedentary lifestyle. The best way to fix this is by taking small steps such as:

- Going for a daily morning/evening walk.//
- Doing housework or gardening. Gardening is also said to heal one's mind.
- If watching TV you can keep moving around the room.
- You can start cycling, try yoga or try a home workout.
- Adopt a pet and take them out for walks and playtime.
- You can even get home workout equipment such as a treadmill or weights.
- Opt for the staircase instead of the elevator.
- Try to have standing meetings in a conference room.
- Start walking to work if it's not at a very far distance. If traveling by train, stand.

- At your workplace try and take frequent walks, especially during lunch breaks.

- Invest in a standing work desk.

Physical self-care is not just limited to a woman who has overburdened herself with responsibilities. Sometimes a person's work can be so exhausting that they completely forget about having a personal or social life which can lead to a sedentary lifestyle. As we have seen above, a sedentary lifestyle is far from a healthy one. What one needs to figure out is how to strike a balance between work and life i.e a work-life balance.

All of the information in this book sums up to two words and they are work-life balance. Work-life balance means treating all parts of your life like chapters in a book. Your work should be one chapter and your family should be another. Imagine reading a book where out of ten chapters 6 are about the same topic. You would get bored, right? Similarly, in your life, your career cannot take up 6 chapters. You are here to live life and while work is important it is not everything. Similarly, while being a mother or a wife is a blessing it cannot define your entire life. There has to be a chapter about yourself and only you can write it. Physical self-care also includes pursuing one's hobbies or doing extracurricular activities. Personally, for me, I love to swim and hike and in the past, I have also tried my hand at karate. I love to spend time in nature and also enjoy traveling. One of my favorite trips was when I went hiking and snorkeling in Australia. These were some of my best habits however, where I went wrong was when I pushed myself too hard and ignored my body's own needs and limitations.

I would also like to touch upon decluttering and the benefits of living a minimalist lifestyle. There have been numerous studies that show that clutter or too many things in our life add to the stress. A minimalist life is one in which a person removes anything excess from their life. You can start with decluttering your house by removing extra utensils, furniture, paintings, books, and anything that you feel is never used and simply takes up space. It also includes decluttering clothes that you have never worn and never will, wearing simple clothes, and not buying anything extra. Subconsciously, this clutter makes our minds cluttered and we do not realize it but it ends up giving us anxiety. By donating these you are doing yourself and someone else a huge favor. A minimalist lifestyle is not limited to donating the extra material goods in your life. It also means removing any habit in your life that is not doing you any good. For example, too many sugary snacks, carbohydrates, etc. Did you know that all monks follow a minimalist lifestyle? They have only one or two pairs of clothing that they always wear, they shave their heads, have no furniture as they live in hostels, and only have the necessities of life. They have cut off everything that causes stress in life. Now you do not have to become a monk but there are various other ways by which you can practice minimalism including:

- Shop quality instead of quantity. When you go shopping don't buy the many t-shirts that are on sale and will go bad in 6 months instead go for the good quality sustainable t-shirt that will last longer.

- Try to digitize your movies and books.
- Bring your coffee mug to your cafe, this way you are helping the planet as well.
- Before purchasing something always ask yourself "Do I need it?"
- Don't be a shopaholic i.e shopping should not be a stress buster for you as it will only waste money and add to the clutter.

There are numerous benefits of following a minimalist lifestyle such as

1. You will save more and spend less. You can then use this money for more valuable experiences such as travel.
2. A home with less stuff is always one with lesser stress.
3. It is way easier to clean a less cluttered home.
4. You will find that not being tied down by material goods has made you freer.
5. It is very good for the environment.

6. The more things we have the more time we waste.

7. Your kids will learn the value of quality over quantity.

8. You can save up and buy better quality goods that will last longer.

9. Minimalism guarantees happiness.

10. You will never compete with anyone as you realize the importance of owning only what is required.

11. A clean minimalist home is very visually appealing.

12. By decluttering some of your old things you will also move on from the past.

13. You will be able to find things very easily in your home.

14. You will have more time to rest.

15. What you will have on display is what you value the most and you will get a chance to showcase it.

A minimalist lifestyle is not for everyone however, it is highly recommended because it is a very easy way to declutter your mind and save lots of money. Do consider this lifestyle for your self-care and if not you can always still remove excess things from your home and donate.

Chapter Activity:

Write down your favorite forms of physical activities and the ones you wish to learn. Now beside them write down how many minutes you can spend every day doing these activities.

Read the paragraph below after completing the activity.

You will realize that you are willing to learn and give time for physical activity every day and the only thing stopping is motivation. So start today and go for that dance class or go for a swim, do whatever makes you feel great about yourself. The only delay is you not taking that first step.

Chapter 3:

Mental Self-Care

Love yourself first, and everything else falls in line. You really have to love yourself to get anything done in this world. –Lucille Ball

I feel glad that we live in a world where at least now mental health is being discussed and given importance. Many people have lived their entire lives without releasing childhood trauma or any other kind of trauma and they took this to their other relationships. Mental peace is equally if not more important than physical well-being. Anxieties and depression are on the rise because of competition to survive and also because of technology. We must realize that mental self-care is possible and that it can be the key to many of our problems.

Mental self-care means self-awareness. It is realizing our flaws and strengths and then using those strengths to eliminate our flaws. If you were in a bad relationship where you got cheated on then it can leave you feeling insecure in the next one. Or if you got bullied in school then you can grow up judging people or being insecure about yourself. All of us have some kind of trauma and somewhere we know what it is. You can take a diary and write down what your unhealed traumas are to get better clarity or you can even visit a trusted psychologist who will guide you and give you that required clarity. Apart from unhealed traumas, mental peace also means not being overworked. I am reiterating the book example that we discussed in the previous chapter. Your work, family life, relationships, etc. need to be a chapter in your book and not take over your entire life.

Let's expand on the above relationship example, let's say you got cheated on and now you are left insecure and untrusting of the entire male gender. Now a nice man comes into your life and he is completely different from your ex-boyfriend. In an ideal scenario, you should move on from the past and be happy with this new man. However, an unhealed trauma can cause you to become insecure, jealous, suspicious, and sad for no reason in this current healthy relationship. This is not fair to you or your new partner. Traumas can take over your life and then ultimately even cause hindrance in your work. We all know when we are not on the right path and mental self-care simply means to recognize those and then fix them.

There are also daily habits that you can incorporate into your life to keep your mental peace in check:

- Start by going to bed early and waking up early. We should also try to wake up without alarms as that only disrupts sleep.

- Soaking in the early morning sun can be very good for your health and it also gives you vitamin D.

- Use aroma candles such as lavender or frankincense that are known to aid in relaxation.

- Start maintaining a journal. Everyday journaling leads to clearer thoughts and you can also help plan ahead for the next day.

- Become a plant parent. Not only do they give your house a makeover they also help in keeping the air clean. Taking care of plants and watching them flower and grow is great for one's mental health.

- Follow your hobby or if you're not sure of your hobby then try everything till you find something you truly enjoy doing. It can be knitting, painting, gardening, learning to play a new instrument, etc. I personally love to draw, play the guitar/piano and learn new things. Currently, I am learning different languages including coding languages. I consider myself to be a nerd and I love reading books. Don't worry if you're unsure about a hobby, trust me, try everything, and one day something will click and you will fall in love with an activity.

- We are social creatures and we need other humans to survive. Remove the toxic people from your life and start hanging out with people who want the best for you. You can always spot a person who is not good for you by simply noticing your behavior around them. Are you extra guarded? Do they believe in things that do not align with your morals? It is very important to have good company around you.

- Practice self-care activities like putting on a face pack. You do not even have to invest in one, many face masks can be easily made with home products. For example, take a spoonful of coffee and honey. Mix them and apply them to your face gently, then wash them after 15-20 minutes. This pack is a great exfoliator and will leave you feeling amazing.

- Many of us consume aerated drinks/coffee to keep ourselves energized. However, none of these is good and caffeine is a main ingredient in them which is very harmful to the body. Instead, try and start drinking green tea. Green tea comes in various flavors such as peppermint, strawberry, etc. and it not only is a great replacement but also aids in weight loss, adds to your daily water content, and also makes one feel calm and relaxed.

- Save up and go for a massage. Go for a full body massage or a massage which concentrates on the area of your body that you feel needs stress relief. Massages reduce anxiety, and depression and also help boost immunity.

- Join an online dance class! Dance is an amazing exercise and you must try it out. It will help you lose weight, you will learn some amazing moves for the next time you go clubbing or to a wedding and it's also super fun.

- Many people struggle with saying no. Make it a habit, if you feel that your social battery is running low then say so to your friends and family. Any person who truly supports you will never judge you for wanting to relax.

- Spending time with your pets is another very good way to relax. In case you do not have pets then you can even visit a shelter or dog cafe.

- One of my favorite things that I do to make myself feel better is doing something good for someone else. Give your family or friends a surprise gift and make them feel special and cared for. It will make their day and trust me you will feel amazing.

- Go on a vacation. I love to travel and one of my favorite holidays was in Boston in the US. I fully enjoyed the city, there are four big universities there and you can hear students all around chatting and having fun. There were also tulip flowers in full bloom which were lovely to look at. You must save up and go on at least two trips in a year. Vacations help one unwind and relax and you also get to get out of your comfort zone and meet new people and have new experiences. I also love to hike in Australia and we can snorkel or swim in the ocean with the fish. One of my other favorite things to do is to call my family over and spend some time with them. I love to travel to Vietnam, where my parents are from, and spend some quality time with them. You must spend time with family and go on trips with them too.

- Before going to work or for any important event, plan your day. This way you can avoid any bumps. For instance, anticipate how much time will take you to reach a certain place and then leave. Make sure to eat breakfast so that you are not cranky or have headaches, in case your lunch gets pushed. Planning will make you feel in control which is always good to reduce any anxieties.

- Spend some time in nature every single day. Be it a nearby garden in your area or a sea/lake. It can be any form but it has to be nature. This will help you feel calm and grounded.

- Before sleeping, turn off social media as it only leads to anxiety and can also cause loneliness.

- Orgasms are great stress relievers and an active sex life only has benefits. If you do not have a partner then do not shy away from doing it yourself. Through masturbation, you learn about your own body and needs which ultimately leads to a better sex life as well.

- Make sure your house is clean. You have to take out time to clean your house every single day. Dust and clutter cause mind clutter.

- I get worried when people say they never cry. It is the most normal thing and maybe stressed people do not even have the time to cry. You can watch a romantic/emotional film in case you want to induce it.

- One of the main worries that we all humans have in common is money. Doesn't matter if you're rich or broke, money is stress. You can reduce this stress to great amounts by doing a monthly audit of your financial expenditures. You will find it to be a liberating experience and you can even end up not spending so much the next month because you will be keeping a track of your unnecessary expenditures.

- There are many podcasts in this world and all of them cover various topics. A podcast can make you feel connected to the host and it can be like listening to a friend. Try it and see if it works for you.

- We discussed above that in case you feel it is necessary then you can always start therapy. Do not shy away from it as it will only help you.

- Start donating. It can be money, clothes, books, furniture, etc. anything that you feel you do not need and can help someone else. You will feel immense happiness, I promise.

- Be up to date on your medical appointments and get regular checkups of your eyes, teeth, and any other issues that you face. Do not delay them because you do not have the time.

- Take out time to meet your friends. We always feel amazing after meeting them so plan maybe a game night every week or go out. It will help you and your friends. Go for the birthdays and the celebrations as these tiny things ultimately add up to happiness.

- Daydream! Yes, you read that right. Daydreaming is an indication that our imagination is running well.

- In case you feel you have a habit which does not involve therapy but can't be discussed with your friends or family you can always join a support group. These are people going through similar problems and you all can help each other out and you will also know that you are not alone.

Mental health is very important and it is the little things that we do everyday that make a drastic change in a year. Let's say, for example, there are two people, Leah and Angela, they are both the same age and even live next to each other. Leah is a successful artist and spends around 8-9 hours each day in her studio. Her daily routine includes waking up at 10:00 a.m. getting ready and quickly going to work. She eats her breakfast and lunch every day. After she comes back at around 6:00 p.m. she now has to clean her house and make dinner after which she is so exhausted she has no time left so she watches some Netflix and sleeps. This is Leah's every day. On the other hand, there is Angela who is a working mother and she needs to wake up every day by at least 6:00 a.m to first make breakfast, do her yoga, and then get her kids ready for school. After they have left she cleans and then quickly goes to work. She comes back by 6:00 p.m. and then cooks dinner for the family. Her family has a ritual of going out for an evening walk everyday post which they have dinner and sleep. By this point, you must be wondering why I am narrating these women's lives. It is to explain a crucial difference. While Leah does not have anyone else but herself to take care of, Angela has her children and husband to manage. Yet, Angela makes sure to go out every evening and spend some quality time with the family. This may seem like a small thing but my point is that Angela is making an effort as even though the quality time lasts 30-45 minutes she is still doing it. I can list many activities that can be done to feel better but nothing will work till you actively start making efforts to make changes. Leah does not have a social life and the chapters of her book are dominated by her career. However, Angela's book has her family, her work, and herself. Self-care does not mean making drastic changes. We all cannot afford to join dance classes etc. but like Angela, we can actively try to make small changes so that our lives improve.

I hope that through this chapter you have got an understanding of the importance of mental health and can now actively make those changes which will make you a happier person.

Chapter Activity:

Write down the situations that give you the most stress and then think about why they are resulting in stress. Now, think about the ways you can fix these and you will give yourself answers to your problems.

Chapter 4:

Sensory Self-Care

If your compassion does not include yourself, it is incomplete. –
Jack Kornfield

We have discussed the benefits of physical self-care and so now I would like to delve a little deeper and talk about how caring for each of our sensory organs i.e the eyes, nose, ears, tongue, and skin can benefit us. Our internal systems are maintained and nourished by a healthy diet and exercise. However, we can move a step further and give specific care to these organs, a process which results in extraordinary results. We can use each of these sensory organs to achieve immense self-care, I would like to start with the eyes.

Eyes

Our vision is a miracle through which we can see the world and the world can see us. Unfortunately, nowadays our eyes are fixed on phones, laptops, and television screens which is very unhealthy. It is said that when we look at something we love, our eyeballs expand. The entire body is connected and that is why it is possible to use one organ to heal the entire body. I would like to suggest ways through which we can better care for our eyes and through them achieve self-care as well:

- Take at least 15-minute breaks every 45 minutes while looking at your screens. Staring at it for hours on end can lead to eyesight problems and also cause headaches.

- Apply a warm eye pad on your eyes before bed. Usually, this is done to cure styes but this can be done for relaxation as it helps stimulate tear ducts and also keeps the eyes moist.

- You can use artificial tear drops to keep your eyes lubricated throughout the day.

- Watching a candle or a fire burning can also be very soothing to the eyes.

- Take a walk in the park and observe your surroundings.

- Seeing old photo albums can invoke memories which gives one a feeling of nostalgia.

- Visit art galleries.

- Try your hand at drawing, painting, and sketching. Don't stress about it being perfect and just go with the flow.

- You can also watch some of your favorite movies as they can help you feel relaxed as well.

Nose

The smell is a powerful tool as soothing smells go straight to the brain which thereby relaxes the entire body. Aromatherapy is when essential oils, scented candles, and incense sticks are used to reduce anxiety and depression in people. You can try aromatherapy at home itself. The first thing you have to do is smell different types of scents and see which one works for you. Some might like lemony scents while others may like oceany scents. Some of the ways you can practice self-care through smell are:

- Taking a walk in a park or garden full of flowers. This is a natural and readily available method that requires no expenditure.

- If you want to practice aromatherapy then you can start by purchasing scented candles and lighting them up in the evening or while taking a bath. You can also use essential oils, to practice aromatherapy using essential oils. The best way to use essential oils is by taking a cotton swab and dropping a few droplets of the oil onto it and inhaling it for a few minutes. You can also leave this cotton swab in your room. Essential oils are helpful because they are made from petals, roots, and bark of trees and plants and these smells release good chemicals like serotonin in the body. Aromatherapy is used to heal anxiety, depression, and stress. It also helps relax a person, improves sleep quality, can help improve the lifestyles of people with dementia, reduce headaches, improve mood, reduce inflammation, reduce nausea in person, and also ease pain during ailments. Different scents have different benefits. For instance:

- Lavender: It is the most famous one and helps in relaxation and gives better sleep.
- Rose: It is said to reduce anxiety.
- Clary Sage: It is great for stress relief and reducing anxiety.
- Cedarwood: It is great for the circulatory system to function well and also helps clear airways.
- Cinnamon leaf: It gives a warming feeling and is a great refresher.
- Lemon: Is great for uplifting a person and for revitalizing.
- Peppermint: Is great for energizing.
- Orange: This is great for the digestive system and uplifting mood.

- White Camphor: Reduces depression and improves overall mood.

- Geranium: It is a great calming scent.

One other best way you can achieve self-care through scent is by using scented bath oils, shampoos, soaps, shower gels, and lotions. These will leave you feeling amazing throughout the day and are very easy to follow.

Ears

Ever heard an old favorite song and it takes you to the exact time in life when you used to listen to it? The memories, feelings, and nostalgia come back. That is how strong the sound is. An uplifting song can put us in a great mood while a sad song can make us cry. Instruments like the Tibetan gong and chimes can even be used to produce sounds which are said to calm the mind and soul. Sound can heal a person's deepest wounds and it is the most fun activity to practice in self-care. It is said that music therapy and sound healing can help reduce anxiety, depression, and stress. They can increase memory, reduce blood pressure, reduce pain, lower cholesterol, and even reduce the risks of heart diseases.

Ways that you can practice self-care through sound are:

- You can sit and listen to nature's sounds such as birds chirping, rain, ocean waves, etc.

- You can listen to devotional songs of whichever faith you are of.

- You can invest in sound healing instruments such as singing bowls which are easy to play and help release tension, stress, and anxiety. These instruments also help reduce anger, depression, and fatigue and increase a person's spiritual well-being.

- Go for music therapy: Music therapy is a treatment in which instruments, singing, and creating music help a person and give them therapy. Many kinds of musical instruments particularly help in this treatment, they include pan flutes, tuning forks, drums, harps, and singing bowls.

- Have a conversation with a friend about life or anything else that you love to talk and think about. It can be about movies, music, and any topic that you are passionate about and which makes you feel great about yourself.

Tongue

Stressed spelled backward is desserts. What we eat is who we tend to become and that is why healthy eating is said to impact everything in our lives. The reason we become instantly happy after eating our favorite dessert/meal is that pleasure hormones such as dopamine are released in the body which leads to happiness. If you have had a bad day or are feeling low I would 100% recommend you to eat something no matter how unhealthy but makes you feel good. It is okay to let go sometimes and why not do something which makes us happy? Having said that, there must be a limit to everything we eat as we do not want to unnecessarily gain weight and become unhealthy.

There were three studies done by Professors Raj Raghunathan (marketing professor at the McCombs School of Business, Austin), Rishtee Batra (marketing professor at Villanova University, Pennsylvania,) and Tanuka Ghoshal (marketing professor at Baruch College, City University of New York) where they linked spicy foods to aggression in a person. In an interview, Professor Raj Raghunathan revealed that foods do affect how we feel. I would like to go into a little technicality here, our second brain also known as our gut or gastrointestinal tract is affected directly by what we eat as it influences the neurotransmitters that are released. What are neurotransmitters? They are the messengers that directly carry messages from the gut to the brain. The foods we eat are said to affect our mood and emotions and this is because 90% of our mood regulators aka serotonin receptors are located in the gut. For example, when we eat sugary foods dopamine is released and we instantly feel happy. Similarly, hot foods can increase feelings of pain and discomfort. Foods that have higher calories can make one feel positive and having proteins can make one feel motivated and even improve concentration. Professor

Raj Raghunathan suggested that one should follow a balanced diet and not have anything in excess as it will affect one's moods. He also suggested that one must eat foods that promote good bacteria in the gut. Such foods include fresh fruits and vegetables, foods that are high in probiotic content such as yogurt and kimchi, and overall reducing carbohydrates and sugars (Sawhney, 2021).

One other way to achieve self-care through taste is by practicing mindful eating. This is when you truly sit and taste and enjoy the food you are eating. You pay attention to the flavors, textures, temperatures, and the overall taste and feelings that are released while you are eating your food and avoid any distractions like the TV or your phone.

We all have that one childhood snack that we remember till now and will always cherish. We won't be able to go back to that time but eating your favorite snack/sweet from that time can bring back memories of happiness and relaxation, what childhood was all about. Lastly, I would also recommend you try out various cuisines. Go out alone or with your friends and family to a restaurant you have never been to before and try out different cuisines. You will feel amazing and who knows maybe you'll pick a new favorite.

Skin

Touch is another strong sensory organ which can help us. It can detect all kinds of emotions such as fear, love, comfort, etc. and we can use it to achieve self-care as well. The skin is connected to the brain as well as the central nervous system and hence it automatically can affect our moods as well. Some tips through which you can receive self-care through touch include:

- Spending at least 10/15 minutes once a week exfoliating your feet and pampering them. This can be done by soaking your feet in a warm bucket of water with some salts in it and then using a foot scrubber to remove the dead skin from your feet.

- Walking in the rain or walking by the beach and feeling the touch of nature and the breeze on your skin.

- Applying lotion on your body to give it a nice moisturized feel. You can also keep a small lotion bottle in your handbag and you can use it throughout the day to smell and feel amazing about yourself.

- Putting on a sheet mask or any face mask to feel instantly rejuvenated.

- In the winter put on the heater, wear comfortable sweaters and cuddle up with your blanket to feel cozy, and safe and to get a good night's sleep.

- Never wear tight clothes, especially undergarments. Your skin should be allowed to breathe. You must also not wear uncomfortable cloth material, opt for cotton, polyester, or denim.

- Have a hot shower bath and be mindful of the way the water feels on your skin.

- Dry brushing your skin helps stimulate your nervous system and aids in lymphatic drainage as well.

- Go for massages, and buy a foot or chair massager for your home.

- Set up a skincare routine that you follow every day.

- Hug your family, pets, and friends. Or even better hug yourself!

- Avoid strong soaps on your skin, go for well branded soaps.

- Wash your face throughout the day as it can help you feel rejuvenated.

- Wash your makeup before going to sleep.

- Use the correct skin products, products with green tea, vitamin C, pomegranate, and olive leaf are said to be very good for the skin. We all have different skins so it's best to do a little research on your end as well about which products are best for your skin type. If in doubt visit a gynecologist.

The above self-care routines that I have suggested are easy to follow and some are even fun to do. Trust me that by following any of these you will do yourself a big favor and make significant progress in your self-care routine. For 18 years of our lives, we are dependent on our parents for our well-being but a time does come when we need to start caring for ourselves. Living a full life means caring for ourselves as well, we are the only permanent thing in our lives and so why not treat ourselves like the queens we are? So choose any of the self-care methods that you resonate with the most and start your self-care journey.

Chapter Activity:

For this chapter, my activity for you is to take a walk in the park alone or with your family and truly engage yourself in the surroundings.

Chapter 5:

Creative Self-Care

Keep good company, read good books, love good things and cultivate soul and body as faithfully as you can. –Louisa May Alcott

If there is one thing I truly believe in is that all humans are creative. While platforms like TikTok and Instagram reels have a lot of negative traits, one thing that it shows us is that almost everyone has some or the other talent. The fact that we all have imaginations means that we're creative. If today I get 50 people in a room and tell them to write a story about a dog and an alien, I will get 50 different stories with different genres, storylines, and messages. The only difference between professional creatives and the rest of us is that we never tap into our creativity. Well, we are going to change that with this chapter and I would like to suggest ways in which you too can be creative:

- You can start by practicing creative rest. You can start to do this within your workplace by putting pictures up of your favorite places to visit, foods to eat, activities to do, musicians, etc. The workplace can be a stressful environment but your personal work desk does not have to be.

- Draw/paint/sketch without worrying about how it will turn out to be. Let your imagination flow and see what you create on paper. Use different colors, experiment, and do not be afraid of judgments. You are not here to pass a test, instead, you are simply letting your creative juices flow.

- Write a poem or a story. Many of us might have tried our hand at poetry at some point in our lives, it usually stems from either being in love or heartbroken. Well, you don't have to wait for that. Simply start writing and don't worry about rhyme schemes and the lot. These activities are only for you and who knows maybe they'll turn out really good and you can actually discover a hidden talent?

- Learn to play an instrument.

- Sing out loud your favorite song and just sing without any worries.

- Play your favorite music and start dancing. You can do it alone in a room or you can even join a dance class.

- There are many adult coloring books which have some amazing designs such as mandalas that you can use to color.

- Create a Pinterest mood board. This can be about anything, be it your wishlist of places to travel, the kind of music you like, people who inspire you, your favorite song lyrics, or a combination of all.

- You can try your hand at pottery or use clay at home to make something amazing.

- Watch a funny video online.

- Re-watch your favorite comedy movies.

- Talk to a friend and converse about happy things such as something funny that happened to you recently.

- There is a therapy called laughter therapy where you make yourself laugh till you actually start laughing and this is a guaranteed way to make you feel good. In fact, in many places, there are groups that meet every morning to have a hearty laugh for 15 minutes.

- Try your hand at cooking. Cooking is an art and a very creative profession. Start from scratch and even try plating creatively but don't look for inspiration online. Simply plate according to your own thoughts.

- There are many do-it-yourself videos online and some are really good. Try your hand at DIY lampshades, candles, etc.

- Try a new hobby.

- Redecorate your home or workspace.

- Visit a museum and see the local art.

- Try your hand at classes that can eventually benefit you as well, such as makeup classes, lipstick-making classes, knitting, sculpture class, flower arranging, crocheting, woodwork, calligraphy, etc.

- Journal.

- Learn a new language.

- Learn about a new culture and make plans to actually visit that country.

- If you have a friend who is a professional creative then go to their workplace for a day and help them out.

There are no limits to creativity and you can do any one of the above-mentioned things and you will find yourself happier and more confident about yourself. There are many benefits to embracing creativity which include:

- You get to learn something new about yourself and may even come upon a hidden talent.

- It allows a person to express themselves and to understand themselves better.

- It promotes problem-solving as activities like writing, composing, and drawing are known to bring that out in a person.

- It reduces stress and anxiety.

- It makes one more confident about themselves.

- It increases self-expression and removes any doubts or insecurities one might have about oneself.

- It makes one more creative and this creativity can be used in one's own work as well.

- It promotes thinking out of the box.

- It makes one feel happy.

- One feels pride and a sense of accomplishment.

- If you join a class you can meet like-minded people and actually make some new friends.

- It increases focus and promotes brain health.

- It makes one more of a risk taker.

- It promotes innovation and a person can come up with new ideas.

- It puts one on a journey of lifelong learning which directly means lifelong growth.

- It makes one feel more free.

- If you learn to DIY then you can even save a lot of money.

- It improves one's mood.

- It improves cognitive function because when we are creative we use parts of our brain that usually do not come into function.

Did you know that musicians have better cognitive functioning because they develop better complex problem-solving skills, logical reasoning, and conceptual tasks. Never say that "I am not creative" just because you have never tried your hand at it. Remember when we were kids? We used to draw, sing, and play without any inhibitions because no one had told us that we were not creative. So try your hand at creativity and see how it improves your overall self.

Chapter Activity:

Take a writing pad and try to write a short 300-word story where you are the main character and you go on an adventure, write in detail about the things you do, places you visit, and the people you meet. This is a great task to tap into your creativity and find things about yourself that you didn't know.

Chapter 6:

Emotional Self-Care

With every act of self-care your authentic self gets stronger, and the critical, fearful mind gets weaker. Every act of self-care is a powerful declaration: I am on my side, I am on my side, each day I am more and more on my own side. –Susan Weiss Berry

While we may have commonly heard of the terms physical health and mental health, emotional health is a subject that is hardly touched upon. If it were up to me I would introduce a subject in all the schools in the world where topics like emotions, feelings, and vulnerability are openly discussed. So what is emotional health? One of the best definitions I have come across about emotional health is "Emotional health is about how we feel about ourselves, how we handle difficult situations, and how we acknowledge both our own and other people's feelings."

(Ertel, 2021).

Emotional health is basically your mental health as it affects how you react in stressful situations and the highs and lows of life. You must have heard of the term emotional intelligence or emotional quotient. It is when a person is able to appropriately handle their own emotions even in stressful situations and is also able to empathize with other people. Someone with a higher level of emotional intelligence will be able to read a room better and be able to understand and empathize with even a stranger instead of immediately judging them. Emotional intelligence can be developed as well and being a person with a high EQ means a person who can get along well with people as they can empathize with them, a person who is aware of their shortcomings and strengths and can work on their weaknesses, a person who has high moral values and high ethics which they use in their work, business, and relationships, a person who understands the reason for their reactions and emotions such as anger, frustration, etc, a person who is present at the moment instead of being stuck in the past or worrying about the unforeseen future and a person who is very aware of their boundaries for instance, being aware of when to say "no" to someone.

We can all strive to become better with our emotional intelligence as that will not only help us empathize with others but also with ourselves. While the topic is self-care for emotional health I do believe that first, we must strive to improve our general emotional health and emotional intelligence as well. You can easily develop better emotional intelligence by doing the following:

- Put forward your opinions/ ideas respectfully and without hurting other people's emotions.

- If in a situation of conflict reacting with anger or irritation is common however a person with a high EQ will try to find a resolution instead of increasing the problem even more.

- Be mindful and always be a good listener. Usually, people are just waiting for their turn to speak but it is when we listen that we can learn better. So be a good listener, understand, and then speak.

- Be a motivated person, be self-motivated about self-improvement.

- Try and always have a positive attitude, you can do this by practicing meditation, surrounding yourself with motivational quotes on your work desk, or having a fun lunch/dinner.

- Try being more observant of other people's body language, way of talking, and emotions as that will make you a better communicator. You should be able to read a room better.

- If you are criticized or made fun of, do not take it to your heart and instead understand why the person said so. If you logically agree then incorporate those criticisms into your life and try to be a better person and make those changes otherwise simply ignore them.

- Start empathizing with others before judging or shutting them down.

- Develop your leadership skills by taking on challenges and becoming a reliable person.

- Become more sociable and approachable. Become a person who people are comfortable with.

- Connect with yourself and take a pause and think about why you are feeling the way you are.

- Pay more attention to your behaviors as well as extreme emotions.

- We are often in our own "opinion bubble" and questioning our own opinions is a healthy exercise for developing a higher EQ.

- Always celebrate when something positive happens in your life but do not let it get to your head.

- Understand why you are feeling negative and then work on it.

- Understand your emotional triggers and work on removing them from your life.

- Trust your intuition as it is always right.

- Try to be more curious about people and other cultures.

- Stop complaining and start living.

- Never give in to peer pressure.

We all have had moments where we said something in anger that we instantly regretted later and some people even go to the extent of using physical violence in even minute problems. Those people are unable to control their emotions but that does not mean they never will be able to. Life is all about growth and learning from past mistakes. If you are actively trying to be a better person then you are already emotionally healthy.

One of the biggest ways in which emotional health is affected is when a person is in a bad relationship and they do not necessarily have to be with a partner; it can be with toxic friends, families, colleagues, etc. These kinds of relationships can emotionally scar a person and make them vulnerable, and insecure and put them in a place of great sadness. That is why I would suggest you get out of those kinds of relationships. Those who are suffering know that what is happening to them is wrong however they are unable to get out. All you need is strength and you can run away from those relationships as explaining or reasoning with the people hurting you is unfortunately, next to impossible. The first step to understanding our emotions is to not suppress them and let them out. Be it sadness, anger, anxiety, etc. first let it out and then work on understanding why you are feeling the way you are after which you can move to a resolution.

There are many self-care activities you can practice to support your emotional health and they are:

- Be who you are and do not be afraid to be the person you are no matter how eccentric. If you love to dress in bright colors then do so! Or if you love to wear no makeup then don't. Never give in to societal pressure especially when it takes away from the person you are.

- Learn to be vulnerable. We are not living in a superhero film where everything is under control. If you feel exhausted or overwhelmed then vent to your mother/partner/friends or whoever you feel comfortable with.

- Never be in a relationship where there is only you giving and never receiving as they end up being emotionally draining.

- Do not be a waste bin for someone's emotions. These people are always complaining and are also known as energy vampires as they know that you will listen to them no matter what. Avoid them completely and be with positive emotionally mature people.

- Hugging releases the oxytocin hormone if done beyond 10 seconds. So go hug your family now!

- Start journaling.

- If something is bothering you or a person is irritating you, you do not have to necessarily react at that time. Let things cool down and then react calmly.

- Stop constantly discussing news/politics or things that are beyond your control. Often these things are over-sensationalized and do not require your energy.

- I would like to reiterate about being grateful as it keeps you grounded.

- Always be open to asking for help.

- To the right people, give love unconditionally.

- Always put yourself and your needs first.

- Start paying attention to your body and its needs.

- Remember to never talk down or negatively about yourself as that ultimately affects your emotional health.

- Practice meditation.

- You can always get help from a coach or a professional in mental health if you feel that is necessary.

- Always take time out to rest.

- Allow yourself to receive positive vibes.

- Learn to accept a compliment.

- It's ok if you make mistakes, everyone is struggling. That's life!

- If you feel you do not have a healthy support system then you can create one. First, become emotionally intelligent yourself and you will see that you attract good people toward you.

- Exercise daily.

- If possible, completely quit alcohol as it is completely unnecessary in life.

- Try to be someone who is always resilient.

- Find your purpose and work towards it.

- Find a coping method that is personal to you and can be used in times of stress.

- Set boundaries for yourself and when you're sure about your boundaries, everyone around you will be as well.

- Love yourself and practice self-compassion.

- Find something you love to do and do it every day, if this can be your work nothing better.

- Stop apologizing and accept that it's ok if you made a mistake.

- Listen to calming music.

- You can also try a meditation app as it helps keep a track of your progress.

Don't fear if you feel that you have very few or none of the aspects of an emotionally healthy person. You can easily develop them by being a little more mindful and the fact that you are reading this book is a guarantee in itself that you wish to improve and love yourself.

You will often hear people say that material possession should not be life's purpose etc. however I disagree with that. You must strive towards whatever you think will make you happy. If it is a private jet then so bit it or a million clothes then that is fine as well. The key to a happy life is to have all those things and yet be detached from them so that if you lose them you do not completely shatter and that is what emotional well-being is all about. It's about being aware and in control of your emotions. I know that after reading this book you will be an even more evolved person and I hope that I can give you the answers that you're looking for.

Chapter Activity:

Please take a blank white sheet of paper and draw a happy person, this person should be firstly your gender and age and should be what you think is the epitome of a happy and satisfied with life person. Feel free to draw their surroundings, who they are with, what they are doing, what they are wearing, their profession, what all they have in terms of material possessions, or any other detail you feel is necessary. Make sure you take at least 10-15 minutes to draw the details. Don't overthink it and simply draw.

Read the paragraph below after finishing your drawing.

The result is what you wish to be or can be. You might notice that there are things you have included that you do not have yourself but somewhere you wish to have. Now circle the things that you have in common with this person; it can be the surroundings, material possessions, people they are with, etc., and notice the uncircled parts. If you feel that you do not have a life purpose then your answer is right in front of you. Those uncircled bits do not have to be the ultimate life purpose for you but they are things that you wish to have but don't, things that will make you emotionally happy when you do have them. Having a purpose or multiple purposes in life is what makes life fun and interesting.

Chapter 7:

Social Self-Care

It's okay to take time for yourself. We give so much of ourselves to others, and we need to be fueled both physically and mentally. If we are in balance, it helps us in all our interactions. –Faith Hill

Social self-care is when a person develops their well-being by developing both their social relationships and their own identity. Social self-care also means surrounding yourself with people who help elevate you while they elevate themselves and removing those people who stop you from being the best version of yourself. It is very important to surround yourself with people who are motivated, real, self-improving, and have the same ethics as you.

Two common sayings that you will often hear are "You're only as good as the company you keep" and "Birds of a feather flock together." (Sonnenberg, 2020).

This is because whether we realize it or not, the friends, family, and colleagues that we have will always affect the way we think in some way or the other. You can notice this growing up, often the biases that our parents have translate directly to our own beliefs even though they are wrong. It is only when we grow up do we realize that we have a biased opinion and can then work on changing it. You will see that teenagers who hang out with other teenagers who smoke, party, or drink will tend to start doing the same. Similarly, many times even the way we speak changes according to how our surroundings talk.

Our company is not limited to people we know but it can also be about our idols and the people in the public light who we look up to. If a person looks up to a sportsperson then they tend to get a few of the habits in their personality as somewhere they want to be like them. Hence, we need to be mindful of the people who we look at as idols as well because subconsciously even that is affecting us. The internet can have a huge impact as well, if we listen to knowledgeable podcasts then we become learners while if we are only watching mindless content on Youtube and Instagram then we will remain unmotivated. The correct people can make you and the wrong ones can break you. Surround yourself with friends who are doing better than you in terms of their careers or relationships. Notice the people who always push you to do better and are your cheerleaders and keep them close. If you are lucky enough to find a teacher or an advisor then look at their positive traits and try to embrace them in your own life. If your family is one that constantly criticizes you and looks down upon you then either confront them or maintain a safe distance. Good company is crucial in life:

A good company can motivate you to work harder and can even make you a better person. For example, if your friend is very passionate about something and they work towards it, their good qualities will automatically rub off on you and you too will become motivated. Similarly, if you surround yourself with a friend who only talks about their problems or relationships then not only will you gain nothing but it is also in some way draining you of your energy. If you have grown up with loving parents who not only loved you but whose relationship was also full of love, respect, and trust then you will see relationships in the same light.

There are many benefits to a supporting company be it in any form, family, partner, colleague, friend, or advisor and they are:

- You will feel confident about yourself as you know someone has got your back.

- When you surround yourself with positivity then your mindset becomes positive which leads to motivation.

- Having good company means having people to share the joys of life with.

- You are guaranteed to succeed because you have that support system.

- Through a good company, you will become an extrovert and more outgoing which will open more doors for you.

- Friends are like stress busters and together you all can keep each other away from the tensions of life.

- You will always have someone to go to for advice.

- You will feel that you are loved which will create more happiness.

- You will feel more fulfilled because even if you struggle in some other areas of your life you will know in your heart that at least you have a strong support system.

- You will never feel lonely.

- You will learn more about the world and how it works.

- You will have someone to fall on when you go through a difficult time.

- Healthy relationships can help you leave unhealthy habits.

- Healthy relationships will help you keep your life light and full of fun and humor.

However, remember that to receive all of the above you must be willing to give all of the above as well.

We need people to survive and with good company, life becomes 10 times better. I would like to now share some social self-care tips for you to have a fulfilling and thriving social life:

- The easiest thing to do is to always be in touch with your friends. If they don't call, you can catch up with them about their life and share about yours too.

- Be more social and outgoing. Plan hangouts, getaways, and vacations with your people.

- Volunteering is a great way to meet new people and also do something good for someone. It can be at an old age home, animal care center, or anything you feel strongly for.

- An online forum can help you meet like-minded people and is a great way to discuss topics you might not be able to with your immediate ones.

- Any sort of hobby class such as a cooking class, book club, pottery class, etc. is a great way to increase your social energy and to also learn something new.

- Go on walks with groups who already do, and if not create your own!

- Go out with friends to a new restaurant, movies, and other fun activities.

- Check out a farmer's market.

- Make efforts to connect with your co-workers, who knows maybe they were waiting for you to take a step forward too.

- You can also join group therapy if you wish to.

- Start going to a gym with an already committed gym freak friend.

- Learning a new language is a great way to meet people.

- Make a DIY gift for your friend.

- Go bird watching.

- Go hiking.

- Go on vacations with some of your favorite people.

- Go to a yoga class.

- Arrange a potluck dinner.

- Have fun with your pet or go to a dog park/cafe.

- Set boundaries with your friends etc. so that there is never a conflict. But remember to not cross them yourself.

- Take yourself out to eat or for a movie.

- Go on a solo trip, here you can meet new people from different parts of the world. You can even try to go on a cruise. It is the perfect place to socialize as there are so many activities that bring people together on a cruise.

- Go for a pampering session with your girls, your sister, mother, or daughter.

- Keep in touch with your parents and siblings.

- Become a pen pal with someone.

- Get a life coach in case you feel you need one.

- After work, leave the tensions outside your door and step in to have a fun time with your family. Always remember the book and chapter analogy that I spoke about in previous chapters.

- Have fun! Be a fun-loving and joyful person.

It is okay to feel lonely or isolated sometimes but remember that you can bring yourself out of it if you truly want to. There are more good people in this world than there are bad and you will find them. So let loose and start trusting people more and live a simple carefree life.

Chapter Activity:

Connect with that friend or family member who you have not spoken to in a while and talk to them about this book you're reading and other events in your life or plan a night out with your friends, decide the venue, the date, and everything!

Chapter 8:

Spiritual Self-Care

Self-care is so much more than a beauty regimen or an external thing you do. It has to start within your heart to know what you need to navigate your life. A pedicure doesn't last, but meditating every day does. –Carrie Anne Moss

This may be the last chapter of the book but I believe that spiritual self-care is the most important form of self-care there is and one that must be practiced by all humans to create a more loving and happy planet. Spirituality is a wide term and it can mean different things to different people. For some it can be following the path of a particular religion i.e Christianity, Hinduism, Buddhism, etc, for others, it might be simply believing that there is a higher power but without a particular name, for others, it might mean helping others and being a good person. All religions teach us to love and have compassion for ourselves, for others, and for nature. Spirituality is like self-care for the soul, the soul is what keeps us alive and it is what we truly are. Spirituality also comes in various forms; it can be in the form of prayer, meditation, journaling, and yoga among many others. Spirituality makes us a part of something bigger and also makes us a part of a community of like-minded people who are trying to find their purpose. Spirituality is important because it promotes the well-being of everything including the planet, ourselves, our neighbors, animals, trees, and everything that the universe is made of.

The importance of spirituality is an endless list but I would like to list a few of them below:

- Spirituality teaches you compassion.
- It teaches you to find a higher purpose and to believe in the unknown.
- It gives one hope.
- It gives one peace.
- It gives one clarity.
- It gives one confidence.
- It teaches about self-control.
- It builds self-esteem.
- It helps you understand the experiences you have had in life better.
- It can even promote faster healing because of the inner strength that spirituality gives a person.
- You become part of something big and also become part of a community which can help you.
- You realize the importance of self-care.

- You actively try to build better relationships.
- You never try to hurt someone or do something unethical.
- You live a life full of morals.
- You become mindful.
- You become grounded as you understand that there are bigger things at power.
- You move away from negativity and move towards the light.
- Your tensions, anxieties, and stress are released.
- You become more accepting.
- You become more forgiving.
- You become empathetic.
- It even makes you sharper as you get clarity and so it can improve your problem-solving skills.
- It becomes easier for you to overcome hardships.
- It can make you live longer.
- You become more grateful.
- You will feel more compassion.

- You will be filled with love.
- It reduces symptoms of depression, anxiety, and stress.
- It improves the immune system.
- It lowers blood pressure.
- You become more outgoing and can connect with people better.

And the list goes on! I do see a shift in people especially in millennials and gen z as they are shifting towards spirituality a lot. I feel that spiritual practices should be a part of everyday life just like drinking water or bathing. Before jumping into self-care techniques for spiritual care I would like to go a little deeper into the types of spiritual practices and how you can incorporate them into your daily life.

There are various kinds of spiritual practices and I would like to explore some of the more popular ones with you below.

Meditation

"Mindfulness meditation isn't about letting your thoughts wander. But it isn't about trying to empty your mind, either. Instead, the practice involves paying close attention to the present moment—especially our thoughts, emotions, and sensations—whatever it is that's happening." (Gelles, 2019).

Meditation is to go within, it is to connect with our thoughts and to focus and concentrate on our inner being. Meditation has various forms and some of the more famous ones include:

Mindfulness Meditation: This meditation is about sitting alone with your thoughts and letting them pass without judging them. You can practice it in a quiet corner of your house sitting on the ground with your eyes closed and focusing on your breathing. Some people become so skillful that they can meditate even while traveling or in other public places.

Transcendental Meditation: This meditation is done by choosing a mantra, a word such as "Om," a phrase, or even a sound. You sit on the ground with your eyes closed and repetitively repeat your chosen mantra. You can start with Om or some other phrases and mantras including focusing on the aspect of your life that you wish to improve. For instance: "May my life be full of joy, peace, and calm." "May my self-destructive habits such as overthinking and drinking completely vanish." "May I achieve spiritual awakening" etc. There are also mantras in every religion that can be used. For example, in Christianity there is Maranatha, Come Lord, or The Lord Cometh. In Hinduism there is Om Shanti Om or Om shanti shanti shanti, here shanti translates to peace. In Buddhism, there is "Om Mani Padmé Hum," and many more (Team, 2019). There are endless mantras and you can go for the ones that you resonate with the most.

Guided Meditation: In this meditation usually a teacher is present but you can find many guided meditations online on Youtube as well. You sit in a relaxed position on the ground, close your eyes and focus on a picture. Some even focus on a white light and concentrate on their breathing, smell, sounds, and textures.

Vipassana Meditation: In this meditation, you sit on the ground with your eyes closed and focus on the physical sensations of the body. It is a 2500-year-old practice and it is said to connect your body with your mind.

Metta Meditation: This meditation is focused on saying kind and loving words to yourself. For example, "May I be at peace." "May I be healthy." "May I find mental clarity." "May I always be safe." "May I always be happy." etc. You sit in a relaxed position and close your eyes after which you take a few deep breaths after which you begin to say the above affirmations slowly and steadily. After some time you focus on a picture in your mind of a close family member or friend who has always supported you and say replace the "May I" with "May you."

Chakra Meditation: This form of meditation also dates back to India. Chakra means wheel and it is said that there are 7 main chakras in the body in different regions. In this meditation, you focus on these chakras and their colors. You can also keep crystals and incense sticks around you to feel better as well.

There are many more but the above meditations are good to get started on. I would also like to share with you the benefits of meditation:

- Meditation makes a person more kind and empathetic.

- Meditation increases focus.

- Meditation makes one feel calm and centered.

- Meditation solves problems like anxiety, stress, and tension.

- Meditation improves problem-solving abilities.

- Meditation makes one relaxed.

- Meditation increases attention span.

- Meditation can cure headaches, migraines, or any other stress-related disorders.

- Meditation can help with postpartum blues.

- Meditation increases a person's resilience to pain.

- Meditation can help people struggling with ADHD.

- Meditation can make you more motivated.

- Meditation can even help your relationships as it will make you calmer.

- Meditation is very good for the general health of a person.

- Meditation makes one more self-aware.
- Meditation can help or prevent memory loss that comes with age.
- Meditation can make you kinder.
- Meditation can make you more accepting as it increases compassion.
- Meditation can help you with any addictions you might have.
- Meditation can improve sleep patterns.
- Meditation can reduce blood pressure.

Meditation is a must in everyone's life and even practicing 15 minutes a day can make huge life changes in your life.

Yoga

Yoga is derived from the Sanskrit word "yuj" which means "to join." Yoga is a movement practice where different body movements are performed and these movements are said to bring harmony between the body and the mind. There are various forms of yoga and each has its asanas or postures which promote mind, body, and spiritual well-being. A few types of yoga include hatha yoga, Vinyasa Yoga, Ashtanga Yoga,

Power Yoga, Jivamukti Yoga, Iyengar Yoga, Anusara Yoga, Sivananda Yoga, Viniyoga, Kundalini Yoga, and Yin Yoga among many others. You can start with basic forms and then slowly move to more experienced techniques. I would recommend joining a yoga class instead of seeing the videos on Youtube as one wrong posture can be harmful to the body.

There are many benefits of yoga including:

- It can promote weight loss, especially practices like power yoga.
- It improves blood circulation which results in better skin and delayed aging.
- It boosts stamina.
- It is very good for gut health and digestion.
- It boosts fertility and reproductive health.
- It promotes better sleep.
- It makes you feel happy.
- It can improve concentration.
- It reduces stress.
- It also helps improve immunity.
- It makes one more flexible.
- It improves one's mental health.

- It reduces inflammation.
- It will increase your strength.
- It will improve your cardiovascular functioning.
- It will help a lot with your self-esteem.
- It will improve bone health.
- It will give you a better posture.
- It will help with burnout, an essential in the lives of busy women.
- It is very good for the spine.
- It is good for joints.
- It helps lower blood sugar levels.
- It also lowers cortisol levels.
- It balances your nervous system.

You can try out yoga as it promotes spiritual growth and the overall well-being of your mind and body.

Tai Chi

Tai Chi originated in China and it is all about movement which promotes the health of the mind, the body, and the spirit. It is fairly easy to learn and will give you lifelong benefits. It is a form of moving meditation and it combines gentle movements that connect your body with your mind. It is slow and circular and is about making the life force flow easily through your body. There are various styles and some include the Chen style, Yang style, Hao style, Wu style, and Sun style (Lam, 2018). This exercise is also best done in a professional class.

There are various benefits of Tai Chi include:

- It helps in weight loss.
- It relieves pain.
- It promotes the cardiovascular health of a person.
- It is great for mental health.
- It improves mood.
- It gives leg strength and balance.
- It boosts the immune system.
- It improves cognitive function.
- It improves bone density which can prevent fractures.
- It helps in getting better sleep.

- It lowers physical, emotional and general fatigue.

The above 3 practices are age-old and numerous people have benefited from them. You must choose at least one of them and make it a lifetime habit. If you do so, you do not have to ever worry about health, peace and not giving yourself self-care.

Some other ways to increase your spiritual well-being and to practice spiritual self-care include:

- Join a spiritual community that talks about your religious or spiritual beliefs.
- Read a spiritual book like the Bible or the Bhagavad Gita.
- Forgive yourself for your mistakes but try not to repeat them. Eventually, you will overcome them.
- Be honest with yourself about your motivations, shortcomings, etc.
- Always celebrate your achievements no matter how small.
- Develop an abundance mindset.
- Try to be non-judgemental.
- Start donating.

- Try solo travel, you can begin with a spiritual place.

- Volunteer at a botanic garden and take your family along.

- Listen to podcasts and other youtube videos on religions and spirituality. I love listening to podcasts on Buddhism.

- Try mindful walking next to a water body.

- Listen to podcasts that talk about the meaning of life.

- Start going to a religious service once a week. You don't necessarily have to be religious to visit. It can be a temple, a church, or any other place. You might connect with the community and feel like visiting every week.

- There are many meditation apps that you can use such as headspace.

- Try mindful walking i.e truly feel your surroundings while walking.

- Clean and clear your space.

- Journal.

- Read inspiring books that motivate you.

- Take a social media break now and then.

- Become more forgiving.
- Practice silence.
- Spend some time in your garden.
- Go for a hike.
- Go boating.
- Stare at the night sky and the bright stars.
- Use natural light to light up your home.
- Listen to devotional or motivational music.
- Be at peace with where you are in life currently.
- Never compare yourself with others.
- Always think about the successes in your life and not your shortcomings or your failures.
- Let go when disappointments come your way.
- Find out what you are passionate about by trying different things as we saw in the creative chapter.
- Actively look for opportunities in your area of interest.
- Always be wary of negative people who only want to take advantage of you.

- Always maintain healthy boundaries.

- Be responsible for your actions instead of blaming them on someone else.

- Do not run behind perfectionism instead run behind growth.

- Always accept when you are wrong.

- Take charge of your life.

- Celebrate the wins but treat success and failure the same, never let ego get in the way.

- Try to stay positive in your failures.

- Always be aware of your strengths, and never feel you don't have any.

- Look for the positive people who bring out the best in you.

- Give yourself unconditional love.

- Help children in need or any other people such as the elderly or differently-abled people.

- Teach your children spirituality and bring spirituality into your home.

- Instead of dwelling on the past, think about how you can learn from it instead.

- Always believe everything will work out in your favor.

- Be an open-minded person.

- If you are struggling to forgive someone, write down about them and reach a conclusion.

- Close chapters of life that are no longer benefiting you.

- It is good to forgive but never forget, never be too trusting of a person who has broken your trust once.

- Always look for lessons in any situation.

- Always be kind and you can show this kindness by doing small gestures for people who mean nothing to you.

- Be thankful for each day.

- Be open to receiving love.

- List down things that you would worry less about if you knew there were other people in the world dealing with them as well.

- Always try and gauge possible stressful situations before they happen and then avoid them.

- Always be connected with your family and friends.

- Overcome any self-image issue you have with yourself.

- Always be aware of where you are in life and what is happening. Meditation can help with this greatly.

- Do not judge or assume before you know the facts.

- Try activities like qi gong as they reduce stress and lower your heart rate.

- Practice contemplation.

- Spend time in nature every day if you can.

You may feel that a lot of the above tips are not spiritual, however, spirituality does not only mean chanting and meditating. It also means being mindful and becoming a better individual yourself. Remember, that it is only when we become the best version of ourselves that we can expect others to do the same. I hope that the above tips have helped you and given you more clarity on what self-care is and how you can practice it. As you can see that there are various forms of self-care and if you even do one from each of the above chapters then I can guarantee you life-changing results.

Almost everything will work again if you unplug it for a few minutes, including you. –Anne Lamott

As working women with families we are conditioned to give but the time has now come to give but to ourselves. Be guilt free and start practicing self-care as you will not only be doing yourself a favor but everyone in your life will benefit as well. You will be a kinder and happier partner, friend, mother, daughter, and colleague. All of these people will learn from you and hopefully start practicing self-care themselves. I wish the best for you and give you lots of healing and love from my side.

Chapter Activity:

Go on Youtube and try a guided meditation of at least 15 minutes and feel the difference.

Conclusion

Self-care is the non-negotiable. That's the thing that you have to do. And beauty is the thing that can be the benefit of the self-care. Beauty is not the point. Beauty is just a cute side-effect from self-care. –Jonathan Van Ness

When we have a cup full of tea we will never be able to add anything to it as it will spill, similarly, a person full of responsibilities of careers and families will never be able to include anything else as they will burn out. Self-care is like sugar and when we add it to our teacup it sweetens it. The responsibilities are still there however, with self-care they become very easy to handle. If we have learned anything from the above chapters it is that self-care is not selfish and when we care for ourselves we become better and more productive humans.

Self-care can be as simple an activity as going out and buying yourself flowers, watching your favorite show, changing your sheets, or going out for a cup of coffee. You should not only start following these habits yourself but you must recommend them to your family and friends as well. Imagine a world where everyone focuses on self-care to get better and be better citizens and fellow human beings. It will result in a world that is flourishing and full of love. Self-care does not mean not being ambitious or not going the extra mile for our families. This book is to nudge you to start adding that teaspoon full of sugar to your cup and allow yourself to be happy. Life is long and we need to find ways to make it as easy and relaxing as possible for us. Set a daily time aside for your self-care activities and then dedicate yourself to them. If you want you can also include your partner or friend in some of them to keep you motivated. Start that daily exercise, start focusing on your mental health, pick a hobby you like, start meditating, connect with your friends and family, speak your heart out, dance, sing, travel, and do anything that gives you joy. Remember to take breaks and give yourself time and love.

I would like to end this book with a wonderful poem I came across, it is called "You have to take care of yourself first." I think it beautifully summarizes all that we have learned in the above chapters.

"Little Mortimer Dragon was selfless, heroic, and brave.

He saved me! He is a hero! The villager would rave.

He depleted his energy, lost a large bit of his power.

Came home to nap, eat a bite, revitalize in a shower.

You have to stop giving all of your energy away said is Dad.

If you don't save some for yourself, you will get sick, really bad.

Little Mortimer Dragon had to learn to take care of himself first.

If he had not learned this lesson, his illness might have gotten worst."

(First, n.d.)

Thank you so much for reading this book and I hope that it has helped you in finding the answers you had set out to look for before reading. At the end of this book, I now want you to again think of your priorities and I hope that self-care is now at least in the top 5. I wish you lots of healing and love. If you liked this book do share it with your friends and family as well.

References

The University Of Toledo. (2020). *Self-Care*. Www.utoledo.edu. https://www.utoledo.edu/studentaffairs/counseling/selfhelp/copingskills/selfcare.html

Agarwal, D. S. (2022, November 24). *16 Positive Effects Of Healthy Eating On Your Life*. STYLECRAZE. https://www.stylecraze.com/articles/positive-effects-of-healthy-eating-on-your-life/

becker. (n.d.). *Benefits of Minimalism: 21 Benefits of Owning Less*. Www.becomingminimalist.com. https://www.becomingminimalist.com/minimalism-benefits/

Brennan, D. (2021, October 25). *How Spirituality Affects Mental Health*. WebMD. https://www.webmd.com/balance/how-spirituality-affects-mental-health

Brysha, D. (2020, October 20). *9 Ideas to Add More Creativity Into Your Self-Care Flow*. Self-Care Society. https://myselfcaresociety.com/blog/9-creative-self-care-ideas/

CDC. (2022, September 24). *The Health Effects of Overweight and Obesity*. Centers for Disease

Control and Prevention. https://www.cdc.gov/healthyweight/effects/index.html

Centers for Disease Control and Prevention. (2021a, May 16). *Benefits of Healthy Eating.* Centers for Disease Control and Prevention; U.S. Department of Health & Human Services. https://www.cdc.gov/nutrition/resources-publications/benefits-of-healthy-eating.html

Centers for Disease Control and Prevention. (2021b, November 1). *Benefits of physical activity.* CDC.gov. https://www.cdc.gov/physicalactivity/basics/pa-health/index.htm

cocoshore. (2020, September 5). *Sensory Self-Care Activities: - Cocoshore - Love Your Body - Self-Care.* Cocoshore. https://cocoshore.com.au/2020/09/05/sensory-self-care-activities/#:~:text=Sensory%20self%2Dcare%20has%20the

Dabur. (n.d.). *What is Yoga? Different Types of Yoga & History of Yoga | Dabur.* Www.dabur.com. https://www.dabur.com/amp/in/en-us/about/science-of-ayurveda/yoga/what-is-yoga-and-types-of-yoga

Davidson, K. (2021, May 10). *20 Tasty Fruits with Health Benefits.* Healthline. https://www.healthline.com/nutrition/healthy-fruit#20.-Grapefruit

Delaney. (2022, April 19). *25 Self-Care Ideas for the 5 Senses.* Authentically Del. https://authenticallydel.com/self-care-ideas-for-the-5-senses/

Dowd-Higgins, C. (n.d.). *Emotional Intelligence Part II: 7 Signs of Strong EQ.* Www.ellevatenetwork.com. https://www.ellevatenetwork.com/articles/7300-emotional-intelligence-part-ii-7-signs-of-strong-eq

Earley, B., & Marlys, M. (2022, May 25). *These Self-Care Tips Will Help You Be the Best Version of You.* Oprah Daily. https://www.oprahdaily.com/life/health/g25939272/self-care-tips/?slide=40

Ertel, A. (2021, November 19). *What is Emotional Health?* Talkspace. https://www.talkspace.com/blog/emotional-health-definition/

Esther. (2019, July 23). *16 Simple Ways to Practice Emotional Self Care.* Through the Phases. https://www.throughthephases.com/emotional-self-care/

Ezrin, S. (2017, August 30). *13 Benefits of Yoga That Are Supported by Science.* Healthline. https://www.healthline.com/nutrition/13-benefits-of-yoga#TOC_TITLE_HDR_14

First, Y. H. T. T. C. of Y. (n.d.). *You Have To Take Care of Yourself First by PinkFaerie5.* Allpoetry.com. Retrieved January 31, 2023, from https://allpoetry.com/poem/16923940-You-Have-To-Take-Care-of-Yourself-First--by-PinkFaerie5

Gelles, D. (2019). How to Meditate. *The New York Times.* https://www.nytimes.com/guides/well/how-to-meditate

goodgoodgood.co. (2022, August 11). *98 Best Self-Care Quotes To Remind You What Matters.* Good Good Good. https://www.goodgoodgood.co/articles/self-care-quotes

Greenidge-Horace, R. (2021, April 6). *12 Spiritual Tips For Self-Care To Boost Your Health - Solutions With Rush.* Solutions with Rush. https://solutionswithrush.com/tips-for-self-care/

Guest. (2018, September 8). *Paragraph on Importance of Good Company.* EdgeArticles.

https://edgearticles.com/2018/09/08/paragraph-on-importance-of-good-company/

health line. (2020, June 30). *7 Reasons Why You Should Drink More Water.* Healthline. https://www.healthline.com/nutrition/7-health-benefits-of-water#The-bottom-line

health shots. (2021, June 2). *5 DIY coffee face masks that will nourish and brighten your skin.* Healthshots. https://www.healthshots.com/beauty/skin-care/5-diy-coffee-face-masks-that-will-nourish-and-brighten-your-skin/

Jane. (2015). *22 Ways to Practice Emotional Self-Care and Letting Go.* Habitsforwellbeing.com. https://www.habitsforwellbeing.com/22-ways-practice-emotional-self-care-letting-go/

Jeon, H. (2020, June 17). *A Minimalist Home Can Reduce Stress and Improve Your Well-Being, Experts Say.* Good Housekeeping. https://www.goodhousekeeping.com/home/decorating-ideas/a32824185/minimalist-living/

Kaiser, E. (2020, July 30). *What is self-awareness and why is it important.* Better Kids. https://betterkids.education/blog/what-is-self-awareness-and-why-is-it-important

Krstic, Z. (2020, January 29). *30 Quotes That Will Finally Get You to Take Some "Me Time."* Good

Housekeeping. https://www.goodhousekeeping.com/life/g30693515/self-care-quotes/?slide=2

Lam, P. (2018). *What is Tai Chi? | Tai Chi for Health Institute.* Tai Chi for Health Institute. https://taichiforhealthinstitute.org/what-is-tai-chi/

Leech, J. (2022, January 6). *10 Top Benefits of Getting More Sleep.* Healthline. https://www.healthline.com/nutrition/10-reasons-why-good-sleep-is-important#9.-Affects-emotions-and-social-interactions

Link, R. (2017, May 14). *The 14 Healthiest Vegetables on Earth.* Healthline. https://www.healthline.com/nutrition/14-healthiest-vegetables-on-earth#TOC_TITLE_HDR_16

Mackey, M. (2021, November 1). *100 Quotes About Self-Care, Because Being Good to Yourself Has Never Been More Important.* Parade: Entertainment, Recipes, Health, Life, Holidays. https://parade.com/1070248/maureenmackey/self-care-quotes/

Malige, Dr. M. (2022, February 17). *Obesity In Women: Understanding Dangers Of Excess Fat In Women And How To Maintain Healthy Weight.* NDTV.com.

https://www.ndtv.com/health/obesity-in-women-understanding-dangers-of-excess-fat-in-women-and-how-to-maintain-healthy-weight-2772432

McIntosh, J. (2018, July 16). *15 benefits of drinking water and other water facts.* Www.medicalnewstoday.com. https://www.medicalnewstoday.com/articles/290814#sources

Medline Plus. (2017, June 27). *Health Risks of an Inactive Lifestyle.* Medlineplus.gov; National Library of Medicine. https://medlineplus.gov/healthrisksofaninactivelifestyle.html

Merriam-Webster. (2019). *Definition of BURNOUT.* Merriam-Webster.com. https://www.merriam-webster.com/dictionary/burnout

Miles, M. (2022, May 31). *Why Is Friendship Important in Life? Here's Why.* Www.betterup.com. https://www.betterup.com/blog/why-is-friendship-important

O'Brien, E. (2021, October 6). *Everything You Need to Know About Singing Bowls.* Yoga Journal. https://www.yogajournal.com/lifestyle/fashion-beauty/yoga-gear/singing-bowls/

OASH. (2019, March 27). *Weight and obesity.* Womenshealth.gov. https://www.womenshealth.gov/healthy-weight/weight-and-obesity

Perfomance Health. (n.d.). *Essential Oils Benefits and Uses Chart | Performance Health.* Www.performancehealth.com. https://www.performancehealth.com/articles/essential-oils-benefits-and-uses-chart

Phillips, K. (2020, June 7). *25 Positive Quotes About Self Care.* Country Living. https://www.countryliving.com/life/inspirational-stories/g32772382/self-care-quotes/?slide=13

Rebecca. (2021, October 10). *10 Amazing Benefits of Having Positive Friendships.* Minimalism Made Simple. https://www.minimalismmadesimple.com/home/positive-friendships/

Risser, M. (2022, November 24). *11 Ways to Practice Emotional Self Care.* Choosing Therapy. https://www.choosingtherapy.com/emotional-self-care/

Roche Martin. (2022, January 12). *50 tips for improving your emotional intelligence.* Www.rochemartin.com. https://www.rochemartin.com/blog/50-tips-improving-emotional-intelligence

Roy Chowdhury, M. (2019, June 19). *5 Health Benefits of Daily Meditation According to Science.* PositivePsychology.com. https://positivepsychology.com/benefits-of-meditation/

Sally b's skin yummies. (2021, July 18). *The 10 Best Ways To Take Care Of Your Skin.* Www.sallybskinyummies.com. https://www.sallybskinyummies.com/blogs/blogs/17681905-the-10-best-ways-to-take-care-of-your-skin

Santos-Longhurst, A. (2018, July 18). *The Uses and Benefits of Music Therapy.* Healthline. https://www.healthline.com/health/sound-healing#summary

Sawhney, V. (2021, August 6). *Weirdly True: We Are What We Eat.* Harvard Business Review. https://hbr.org/2021/08/weirdly-true-we-are-what-we-eat

says, D. P. (2021, July 28). *Different Types of Yoga: A Complete Guide.* HealthifyMe. https://www.healthifyme.com/blog/types-of-yoga/

Semeco, A. (2017, February 10). *The Top 10 Benefits of Regular Exercise.* Healthline. https://www.healthline.com/nutrition/10-benefits-of-exercise#TOC_TITLE_HDR_11

Shannon-Karasik, C. (2018, November 13). *25 Ways You Can Practice Self-Care Every Single Day*. Women's Health; Women's Health. https://www.womenshealthmag.com/health/a24886599/self-care-routine-tips/

Sonnenberg, F. (2020, March 24). *You're Only as Good as the Company You Keep — Frank Sonnenberg*. Frank Sonnenberg Online. https://www.franksonnenbergonline.com/posters/youre-only-as-good-as-the-company-you-keep/

speakgoodenglishmovement. (n.d.). *Birds of a Feather Flock Together*. Www.languagecouncils.sg. https://www.languagecouncils.sg/goodenglish/resources/idioms/birds-of-a-feather-flock-together

TeachThought. (2019, November 15). *The Significant Benefits Of Creativity In The Classroom*. TeachThought. https://www.teachthought.com/learning/benefits-creativity/

Team, M. (2019, November 14). *What Is Mantra Meditation? - Match your Intention | Mindworks*. Mindworks Meditation. https://mindworks.org/blog/what-is-mantra-meditation/

Thorpe, M. (2020, October 26). *12 Benefits of Meditation.* Healthline. https://www.healthline.com/nutrition/12-benefits-of-meditation#12.-Accessible-anywhere

thrivemarket. (2016, March 25). *20+ Benefits of Yoga.* Thrive Market. https://thrivemarket.com/blog/benefits-of-yoga

Valerie. (2021, April 5). *15 Fun and Playful Ways to Practice Self-Care.* Families for Depression Awareness. https://www.familyaware.org/15-fun-and-playful-ways-to-practice-self-care/

Weg, A. (2021, September 2). *How Tai Chi Can Ease Pain, Improve Your Balance, and Protect Your Bones.* Prevention. https://www.prevention.com/fitness/a36888559/tai-chi-health-benefits/

Welch, A. (2019, May 31). *A Guide to 7 Different Types of Meditation | Everyday Health.* EverydayHealth.com. https://www.everydayhealth.com/meditation/types/

Williams, K. (2022, September 12). *23 Social Self-Care Ideas to Keep You Engaged and Happy.* Kb in Bloom. https://kbinbloom.com/social-self-care-ideas/

Williams, R. (2019, March 28). *10 Spiritual Self-Care Tips To Be Happy*. Chopra. https://chopra.com/articles/10-spiritual-self-care-tips-to-be-happy

Young Entrepreneur Council. (2018, September 21). *10 Ways to Increase Your Emotional Intelligence*. Inc.com; Inc. https://www.inc.com/young-entrepreneur-council/10-ways-to-increase-your-emotional-intelligence.html

www.ingramcontent.com/pod-product-compliance
Lightning Source LLC
Chambersburg PA
CBHW070308010526
44107CB00056B/2532